TV WITHOUT CABLE:
GUIDE TO FREE INTERNET TV
AND OVER-THE-AIR FREE TV

RONALD PETER

CONTENTS

Prologue...4

Benefits to TV Without Cable...5

Why Does Cable TV Cost So Much?.....................................7

Is TV Without Cable Realistic? 8

How Over-The-Air (OTA) Works 9

I Want to Keep Cable - Can I Still Save Money? 11

Streaming Services...12

Streaming Devices..21

How Do I Watch Sports? 26

Now What? 30

Epilogue..31

Other Books by Ronald Peter 32

PROLOGUE

The thought of abandoning your cable subscription might be frightening, but technology changes everything so fast nowadays...let's embrace the change! I hope this book gives you some new information about choices you can make to watch TV without cable, and that it convinces you to make the leap!

To stay up to date on streaming services and media players and learn news, tips and tricks, please sign up for updates. It's easiest to keep you informed by sending a quick email!

To sign up for updates please visit
http://www.toppingspublishing.com/tvwithoutcable

BENEFITS TO TV WITHOUT CABLE

What are you going to get if you ditch your cable company? First of all, you immediately save money on a monthly basis. You have to do the calculations for yourself, but I have never met anyone who would not save money every month by stopping their cable subscription and moving on to alternative services. In fact, you might actually make money off your own home inventory during this process...

Second, you save space. You don't need the DVD player anymore. You don't need the collection of DVDs either! You can start selling these off and declutter your home, simplifying your lifestyle and clearing your mind. Good outlets for your DVDs are eBay, selling them on Amazon, or yard sales.

The biggest benefit is that you change the way you watch TV. Instead of watching a show every week, you may find it more convenient to wait until a season of TV is over, then binge watch the entire season at once. This way, you don't have any cliffhangers and you can keep the whole story in your mind.

Instead of being a PASSIVE TV watcher, where the TV is turned on as soon as you walk in the door and left on all night, you can become an ACTIVE TV watcher. You can pick which shows you want to watch and when you want to watch them...and that makes watching TV a more pleasurable experience. Normally, when you're watching TV, you're the product. You are a captive audience the networks are selling to commercial broadcasters. Now you're in control again and you can watch whatever you want. And speaking of commercials...

Commercials will be a thing of the past! You don't realize the intense pressure commercials put on you until they're gone. There is always something wrong with you - you're not pretty enough, you're not young enough, buy buy buy.

I discovered this myself when my children would watch TV at other people's houses. Typically, when it's their birthday or Christmas, they have a hard time deciding what they want, because they don't know what's out there in the universe. When they are watching TV somewhere else, every ten minutes there's a commercial. Soon afterward, they mention that they want the thing they saw on TV. An hour ago, they had no idea this consumer item existed, but now they need it like their life depends on it!

The desire to own was implanted in my kids in a few minutes. Imagine what a lifetime of constant bombarding with commercials over and over does to one's mindset. Removing cable helps clean your mind and your soul.

WHY DOES CABLE TV COST SO MUCH?

Cable TV prices started going up when the Telecommunications Act went into effect in 1996. From this point on, unrestricted rate hikes became normal for all cable subscribers. For some industries, deregulation has been a success for the consumer. In particular, telephone rates and wireless rates have gone down a great deal. Unfortunately, cable TV has seen a regular increase in rates.

Since 1996, several separate but related events have combined to overwhelm us. Cable rates have increased dramatically while service levels have gone down. The cable industry has consolidated into a few major providers. The makers of cable television programs and distributors of cable television have merged together, creating a vertically integrated industry. Wireless cable companies have been prevented from direct competition with the existing cable companies, which have denied content to their competitors. The cable industry currently has a near monopoly on the residential high-speed broadband Internet market.

Cable TV prices have been rising at three or four times the rate of inflation. This is the rate for a package that includes ALL the channels. Most of us have a basic or expanded basic cable package - the rates for these packages have risen by over fifty percent. Part of the problem is that cable TV operators don't have a lot of competition. The main competitors are Dish Network and Direct TV, but the two satellite providers have limited market penetration.

On a per-channel basis, prices have increased. Popular channels are no longer part of the regular cable service package; we can only get these channels by subscribing to the higher tiers. Service has deteriorated, giving more money to the cable companies directly out of our wallets. According to the American Customer Satisfaction Index, cable companies "now rank among the worst rated businesses in the history of the ACSI."

IS TV WITHOUT CABLE REALISTIC?

The answer to this question is definitely yes.

With a combination of over-the-air television with an antenna, subscription services, a media streaming device, and sports subscriptions, you can drop your cable provider, save some money, AND WATCH THE SHOWS YOU WANT ON YOUR TV NOT THE COMPUTER! We'll look at each of these options in turn, and educate you on what you can do and what you can't do without cable.

If you're not sure, you can always ease into the waters. You can keep your cable subscription, and just get an antenna, then see what channels you can pick up and what doesn't come in clearly. A little while later, maybe you buy an Amazon Fire TV Stick. After that, you may realize that you haven't used cable in a couple of weeks - maybe you just don't need it!

HOW OVER-THE-AIR (OTA) WORKS

In the ancient days of television, before cable, satellite, and the Internet, the only way for your television to receive a signal was with an antenna. In 2009, the FCC forced all the major broadcast networks to begin transmitting their signals in a digital format instead of an analog format. This digital signal is free. From a consumer standpoint, digital either works or doesn't work - there is no more snow on the screen or rotating the antenna to get the best signal.

One difference in receiving an OTA High Definition broadcast signal and receiving a High Definition signal from your cable provider is that the OTA signal is NOT compressed. The cable provider does a significant amount of compression on the signal to squeeze all the channels over your cable line, but the OTA signal has no such limitation. In most cases, the OTA signal gives a BETTER picture than cable or satellite - you'll notice the improved signal more the larger your television is.

Which Channels are Available in My Area?
If you live in or near a metro area, you'll probably have several channels to choose from, including major network affiliates (CBS, NBC, ABC, Fox, etc.) and PBS. If you live in a rural, you may luck out anyway - you won't know for sure until you look up what signals are around you.

TV Fool (http://www.tvfool.com) uses your address to generate a list of channels around you, where in the city they broadcast from, and the signal strength of the channels.

TV Fool creates a graph and color-coded list of channels organized by callsign, signal strength, and distance. It even breaks out UHF and VHF channels. You'll be able to tell quickly which channels will come in clearly, which will be noisy, and which ones won't come in at all.

Once you have an idea of the channels available to your location, look up the callsigns to see what network they represent.

Choosing the Best Antenna
The quality of your signal reception depends on:
- Where your TV is in relation to the broadcast transmitters
- If you are located in a hilly area
- The size, type and height of the antenna
- The direction the antenna is facing

AntennaWeb (http://antennaweb.org) does a great job of explaining the different types of antenna and the kinds you will see in the store.

An amplified antenna has its own power supply. While a regular, non-powered antenna works well when you live close to a city and close to broadcast stations, an amplified antenna is better if you are running a long cable from the antenna location to your TV, or if your broadcast stations are extremely far away. Amplified antennas can introduce noise into the signals your TV is receiving from the antenna. An amplifier increases EVERYTHING about the signal - the parts you want, and the parts you don't want. It is possible for amplified antennas to amplify unwanted electrical interference.

If you live in an urban area, your zip code is usually enough to determine what kind of antenna you need, and it's likely an indoor omnidirectional antenna will be sufficient. Amazon Basics has 4 different types of indoor HDTV antennas supporting ranges of 25, 35, 50 and 60 miles.

If you live in a rural area, your exact location may be more important, and either TV Fool or AntennaWeb should assist you in more accurately determining your best antenna type. You may get better reception with an outdoor elevated antenna, or an antenna that can point directly at the majority of broadcast stations, but it all depends on where you live.

I WANT TO KEEP CABLE -
CAN I STILL SAVE MONEY?

Although you just bought a book about watching TV without cable, you're still not ready to switch, and you want to keep your cable service. Fair enough! Here are some pointers on minimizing your cable bill:

Stop renting any equipment from the cable company (such as the cable modem) and purchase it instead. This switches a recurring cost to a fixed cost. While this requires you to pay more money up front, you save money in the long run.

Inventory your existing equipment from the cable company and eliminate any cable boxes or other devices that see minimal use. For example, you may not need cable service in the extra bedroom.

Cable companies often have an attractive introductory rate, but once that rate is over, the prices of cable increase dramatically. When your introductory period is over, the simplest negotiating tactic is to call them up and keep saying you want to cancel your service until you get to the retention department. You don't have to get angry - this will make you upset and make the agent on the other end of the line upset. Just say, calmly and repeatedly, that you want to cancel. Remember, you don't need a reason to cancel!

The customer services representatives at retention are always authorized to offer you upgrades to your service or a steep discount to keep you as a customer. If, at any time, they say they will cancel your service, and they have not offered you a better deal, say you changed your mind and you decided to keep your service - it's impossible for you to lose!

STREAMING SERVICES

The Good Stuff

It's legal! You're not doing anything murky with BitTorrent - everything you watch is aboveboard and lawsuit free.

It's flexible! You can watch what you want, when you want it. You're not limited to your house - you can watch on your phone, or anywhere you can get an Internet connection.

It's full of content! Kiss your DVDs goodbye. Never drive out to Redbox again. Streaming services give you access to a lot of content at a fixed price.

It's ad-free! Most paid streaming services are without commercials, so you don't have to waste your time.

The Bad Stuff

Content is not up-to-date. You may be a few shows behind people who are watching live TV all the time.

You always need an Internet connection. If your Internet goes down, or you're at a place with a spotty Internet connection, you won't be able to use your streaming subscription.

Streaming takes up a LOT of data. Depending on your phone plan or home Internet plan, you may hit your data limit. This book is primarily focused on the American market - be glad you don't live in Australia!

The Choices

Following are the most popular streaming services and descriptions of the pros and cons of each service. We all know the pros - we get to watch TV and movies! However, the cons of each service are unique and may not be obvious until you have used the service for a few weeks. The discussion of each service reveals the gotchas so you can intelligently construct a package that best meets your needs.

Netflix

There are three different types of Netflix plans, but for the purposes of streaming, there is only one plan with three different flavors.

The single plan we are focused on for streaming is "Netflix Streaming Plan". The three different flavors are standard definition, high definition with 2 screens, and high definition with four screens. If you want someone to pick a plan for you, you probably want high definition with 2 screens ($9/month).

The standard definition plan is cheapest, but will not look good on a modern, large, high-definition television set. The picture will be blurry. An additional limitation is the single screen - you will only be able to watch from your Netflix account on one device at a time. Perhaps it is a blessing that you can only view a blurry unwatchable video on your TV, and not your TV and iPad.

Now that we've narrowed the plan choices down to two useful plans, the only decision we have to make is if we want 2 simultaneous screens or 4 simultaneous screens. You may be thinking to yourself, "Self, I am a single person..." or "Self, I only have two TVs..." Why would you want the ability to watch 4 Netflix streams at the same time?

You want this ability if you are sharing your Netflix subscription with other people. If you purchase the most expensive HD streaming plan at $12/month, and share it with 3 other people, you are now only paying $4/month for Netflix. This price is unbeatable.

Netflix has a LOT of content, is very easy to use, and since they have been around the longest of all the streaming services, they are compatible with every streaming device out there.

The main problems with Netflix are that movies and TV shows can take a long time to make their way into the Netflix system. Even when a movie or TV show makes in Netflix, it might not be there forever. Netflix licenses all of their content from different studios, and each studio is signed to a contract of varying duration. When a new year begins, it is common for many shows to suddenly become unavailable on Netflix, and new shows to show up on Netflix.

At $4/month, it's worth a shot though, right?

Amazon Prime
I may be showing some bias here, but there are many benefits to using Amazon Prime and no downside.

With Amazon Prime, you get more than free videos and free movies. You get free two day shipping and free music. You are allowed to share your shipping subscription with family members; the description under "share your subscription" says the family members must live in the same household, but in my experience that is not the case. You do need to know the birthdate of your "family member".

Each month, you can borrow one book for free from the Kindle Lending Library. This is different from Kindle Unlimited, which is an all-you-can-read subscription aimed at high volume readers. The Lending Library contains over 500,000 titles, including many New York Times bestsellers.

Kindle Firsts lets you download one of four books each month BEFORE the publication date. The book is either free or at a reduced price. This helps authors build up a fanbase and gives readers a chance to preview a new book on sale - a win-win for both parties.

I talk about ways to get an Amazon Prime subscription for free in Fire TV Stick User Guide: Support Made Easy (http://www.amazon.com/gp/product/B00SGHKGSU).

Hulu

Hulu fills the TV gap of shows that are currently being broadcast. By that, I mean you're in the middle of the TV season and you want to watch new episodes of a show that are still coming out. The other streaming services only offer older shows.

Hulu has a free option and a paid option. The free option only works on a computer, and may be limited to the last few episodes that have aired on TV.

The paid option (Hulu Plus) works across all devices, Blu-Ray, smart TVs, streaming devices, phones, tablets, etc. Hulu Plus offers all current-season episodes of popular shows unless their agreement with the network only allows them to show the last five or six episodes. Hulu Plus also streams in high definition - the free version of Hulu is standard only.

The biggest problem with both free Hulu and Hulu Plus is the COMMERCIALS! One of the big benefits of TV without cable is supposed to be a commercial-free life, but Hulu steals that benefit right back. The most puzzling part is that you even see the commercials when you pay for Hulu Plus! Remember back when cable TV was just starting out, and everything was commericial-free because you were paying to access the channel? Hulu really tries to ding their audience.

According to comScore data, in January 2014, Hulu showed their viewers an average of 80 ads per month. Sometimes it feels like 80 ads an episode! The next highest was Google-owned sites (including YouTube) at 27 ads per month. Let that sink in for a minute - Hulu showed almost TRIPLE the amount of ads on YouTube! Every year the Hulu CEO says that they are thinking about lowering the ad frequency. Unfortunately, anecdotal evidence and empirical observation indicate that the high number of ads from Hulu are not coming down anytime soon.

Another problem with Hulu is that commercials are supposed to be interesting. When you are watching a video through Hulu, it is possible to see the same commercial over and over again. Maybe people are seeing the same ad 80 times in one month! The lack of ad diversity contribute to the overall consumer dissatisfaction with Hulu.

Finally, even with Hulu Plus, you may not be able to see the entire current season of a TV series, or watch a TV show on a device other than your computer. Everything on Hulu depends on the contract they have with the content provider, so if the content provider doesn't want you watching a show on a certain device or at a certain time, you are at their mercy.

iTunes

iTunes lets you buy or rent movies and television shows. If you are buying a piece of content, it's yours - you're not at the mercy of another company that can have there licenses on streaming content suddenly expire. If you have an iPhone or iPad you may already have accumulated a large collection of media in iTunes that you would like to watch on your TV.

The biggest problem with iTunes is that you are locked into purchasing an Apple TV if you want the easiest, highest quality, problem free viewing on your living room TV. If you don't have an Apple TV, every way to see your already purchased content on your TV is a hack.

The simplest hack involves getting iTunes onto your device (via iPad or iPhone), then mirroring the display and audio to your TV through a streaming device. This process has a lot of moving parts, and if any part in the process breaks down, your viewing will be interrupted.

An even more complicated hack is to download your iTunes content, crack the digital rights encryption on your own file, put your iTunes file on a server, then serve up your decrypted iTunes file through a streaming device to your TV. It's about as pleasant as it sounds.

If you already have an extensive iTunes library, you're going to have to bite the bullet and get an Apple TV. If you don't, now is a good time to ask yourself if being at the mercy of a single vendor is bothersome to you.

Vudu

To understand Vudu, you have to understand UltraViolet. To understand UltraViolet, it helps to think about TV without cable from a movie studio's perspective.

When you have a Netflix subscription, you're totally dependent on Netflix to watch your movie, and the movie studio is also dependent on Netflix to get their movie to you. Instead of Netflix serving as an intermediary, wouldn't it be better for the studios to allow you to watch the movie themselves? It cuts out the middleman and, while it probably won't result in savings for you, will result in a larger profit margin for the movie studio.

Another problem for the studios is that consumers are often ripping their own videos off DVDs and BluRay, and putting the decrypted movie file on their home computers. The studios have no control over this file - it can easily be copied to different computers, or uploaded to the Internet. Again, the problem from the movie studio's perspective is a loss of control and a lower profit margin.

UltraViolet is a way for the production studios to make more money, control the content you watch, and make it difficult for you to own the media you purchase. When you walk into a store and buy a DVD, from your perspective you're purchasing a physical product. From the production studio's perspective, you're purchasing a LICENSE to watch a product. This small difference is how we ended up with the UltraViolet implementation.

For users, the way you start with UltraViolet is by creating an account, which makes a digital locker for you. Your movie information is stored magically in the cloud.

There are three common ways to fill your UltraViolet locker.

The first way is to import your old DVDs and BluRay discs to the UltraViolet system - this is called disc to digital (D2D). This was originally done at a WalMart store; it can now happen in the privacy of your own home, but either way the process costs $2. The DVD is not actually converted; there are already copies of each video that participates in the UltraViolet program, and your account is licensed to access the copy. You can see the subtle shift of 'ownership' - before, you owned a physical DVD. Now you don't really 'own' anything - your account and all the media associated with the account are in the hands of someone else. Once the DVD has been loaded into your UltraViolet account, you no longer need the physical disc.

The second way is to use digital UltraViolet codes. These codes are often included with new DVDs and BluRay discs, but are not always used. They can commonly be found on Ebay or given away for free. From the consumer point of view, you're actually buying two products - the physical product and the digital product. From the studio's point of view, they are giving you access to one product in two different ways, and you are supposed to choose one.

The third way is to use Vudu credit. It is quite a lot of work, but you can find Vudu credit on sale at a discount at various Internet sites.

The least common way to get a movie into your Vudu account is to buy a movie directly from Vudu. This is because everything on Vudu is extremely expensive. One movie from Vudu can be comparable to an entire month's subscription from Netflix.

Some of the problems with Vudu are that you don't have any control over the quality of the film conversions. If there is a problem with the digital copy stored at UltraViolet headquarters, there is absolutely nothing you can do.

The problem of you being helpless is actually at the root of all the problems with UltraViolet. Sometimes the incorrect movie gets associated with your account; again, there is nothing you can do.

Sometimes you have loaded the correct movie into your account, but even though the movie is in your locker, you will not be able to access the media you purchased.

Vudu does not have a monthly fee, and is only available in standard definition on tablets and phones.

In summary, if you already have a large physical media collection, and don't mind paying an additional $2 tax per disc you own, UltraViolet may be for you. Otherwise, stay away!

Sling TV
Sling TV was launched in January 2015. It allows you to watch live TV and some cable channels without a subscription; it is offered by Dish Network. The basic service costs $20/month and includes the following channels: AMC, ESPN, ESPN2, TNT, TBS, Food Network, HGTV, Travel Channel, Adult Swim, Cartoon Network, Disney Channel, ABC Family, CNN, El Rey, and Galavision.

Sling TV offers three premium add-on packages priced at $5/month. This fee is in addition to the $20 base subscription.

The add-on packages are:
Kids Extra – Networks include: Disney Junior, Disney XD, Boomerang, Baby TV, and Duck TV.
News & Info Extra – Networks include: HLN, Cooking Channel, DIY, and Bloomberg TV.
Sports Extra – Networks include: SEC Network, ESPNU, ESPNEWS, ESPN Buzzer Beater, ESPN Goal Line, ESPN Bases Loaded, Univision Deportes, Universal Sports, and beIN Sports.

Some observations and caveats:
- $20/month, no commitments. You pay at the beginning of the billing period, the exact opposite of ever other bill in existence.
- Streaming to a computer, TV, phone, tablet, iOS devices, Roku, and Amazon Fire. Noticeably absent are Chromecast and Apple TV.
- Only one stream supported per account.

- The Sling TV stream is delayed by 1 - 2 minutes from a live broadcast over cable television. For example, if you are watching a football game on ESPN over Sling TV, and your friend is watching ESPN over their cable provider, you will be seeing things happen with a delay.
- Sling TV has no DVR ability, it is for live TV only. There is currently no reliable option to watch TV shows that have aired in the past.
- Sling TV is only available in the United States.

STREAMING DEVICES

Apple TV

If you have purchased a lot of content in iTunes already, an Apple TV is a must have. It is the only streaming device that will be able to get your iTunes content onto your TV. If your home is an Apple-only household, you are required to get an Apple TV to easily watch your content on your TV - and it will work like magic.

If there are apps for your other streaming services, they will work and work well. Examples of these apps are Netflix, Hulu Plus, MLB.TV, NHL GameCenter, NBA, Flickr, YouTube, and iTunes, of course. With Apple TV, things just work. Home sharing will allow you to watch videos from your computer on your TV through Apple TV - the only caveat is that your Mac needs to be on for this to work. You can even be in one room on your computer or laptop, and send music to an Apple TV in another room to play music somewhere else in the house.

The problems start when you want to do things outside of Apple's sandbox.

All competing storefronts are locked out of Apple TV. You will not be able to use Vudu, Target Ticket, CinemaNow, MGO, Flickster - all these services are not compatible with Apple TV. Apple TV has a dearth of apps compared to the competition, and there is no App store like on Roku.

The Apple TV will not natively play Amazon Prime video. There is no Amazon Prime app. The workaround is to use an iPhone or an iPad to stream the video to Apple TV via AirPlay. It's a little ugly, but at least there is a workaround! Again, this is not a big deal if you are already invested in Apple's ecosystem of videos.

Some ESPN content may be viewable on your computer, but not on Apple TV if your provider is not listed with Apple TV.

Chromecast

Chromecast is Google's entry into the streaming device market. It can do the basics like ever other stream device (things like "watch Netflix" fall under the umbrella of the basics), but there are some things to take into consideration that are unique to Chromecast.

It can theoretically be powered by your TV's USB port, but that power source is unreliable. To keep your Chromecast on consistently, make sure it is plugged into a wall socket, not powered through your TV.

There are many more apps for Chromecast than for Apple TV because Google made a decision to make their platform more open than Apple.

Out-of-the box, Chromecast does not support local media playback (movies, photos and music you already have existing on your phone or computer), but this functionality can be added through the Plex app. Plex requires another computer to be on and serving up the media you want to play through Chromecast.

You can mirror your Android phone or tablet to your TV through Chromecast, similiar to Apple's AirPlay.

If your TV is HDMI-CEC compatible, Chromecast can do some truly magical things with your TV. Chromecast can be remotely controlled with your mobile phone or tablet. HDMI-CEC allows Chromecast to pass remote functions through to the TV, meaning your phone can act as a TV remote through Chromecast. Say goodbye to purchasing $100 all-in-one-remotes! As a simple example, the Chromecast can automatically turn on your TV and switch the input to itself; changing the TV input can be a major stumbling block.

Chromecast only has a 2.4 GHz wireless receiver. In a nutshell, 2.4 GHz wireless can travel farther but has fewer channels, so the frequencies are more crowded. 5 GHz wireless cannot travel as far but has more channels; this is superior in an apartment setting, where there are dozens of wireless access points all trying to talk over each other.

Modern routers can broadcast simultaneously on the 2.4 GHz and 5 GHz spectrums, but you could run into problems in two cases. First, your router may be set to broadcast only on 5 GHz - perhaps 2.4 GHz is too crowded to use. Second, if your Chromecast is talking to your 2.4 GHz network and all your other devices are on the 5 GHz network, they may not be able to see or talk to each other depending on your router configuration.

Roku/Roku Stick
The Roku 4 costs $100 and the Roku Stick costs $50. Features are similar across both devices, but the Roku Stick is noticeably slower when using the remote to navigate through menus.

The first time you set up a Roku, be prepared with a laptop or a computer. To use the Roku, you need to create a roku.com account, then pair the account to the existing streaming services you use, such as Netflix, Amazon Prime, or Pandora for music. If you have a computer nearby, you can log into the service with your computer, then have Roku display a code on your TV. Enter the code from the TV onto your computer, and your streaming service account will be paired with your Roku account. The alternative is to type in all your streaming service information onto the Roku with the Roku remote, which is laborious at best.

If you have a choice, a wired Internet connection will always be more reliable than wireless for your Roku.

What every other streaming device calls an app, Roku calls 'channels', which is more consistent with a typical TV viewing experience. The openness of Roku (there are tutorials that say "Start your own Roku channel in 5 minutes!") is in sharp contrast to Apple TV, and is evident when you consider that new apps/channels are frequently on Roku first, and take a while to be ported to other streaming devices.

Roku has a lot of different channels, but they are not all good. There are private channels which are not available through the typical Roku interface; these channels can be manually added on roku.com through "Add Private Channel".

One unique feature to the Roku is that there is an earbud jack on the remote which will automatically mute the TV. If your household enjoys both TV and quiet, this can be a lifesaver.

One negative to Roku is that the newest Roku devices no longer have optical audio outputs. If you have a separate audio receiver that does not have an HDMI input, you won't be able to get surround sound. If the previous sentence doesn't make sense to you, you don't have to worry about it!

Fire TV/Fire TV Stick
The full Amazon Fire TV is $99 and the Fire TV Stick is $39.

The major differences between the two are that the Fire TV is slightly faster, comes with a remote that can recognize your voice, has better parental controls, and has 5.1 surround sound and an optical audio output jack. There are some games that work perfectly well on a Fire TV that won't work on a Fire TV Stick because of the processor differences. If you don't care about any of that stuff, the Fire TV Stick should work perfectly for you.

There is an in-depth discussion of the Fire TV Stick in my book Fire TV Stick User Guide: Support Made Easy! (http://www.amazon.com/gp/product/B00SGHKGSU)

The Fire products are the newest of the streaming devices, so they have the most powerful hardware, but have been the least battle-tested.

The best hardware lets Amazon do interesting new things. Fire TV has something called ASAP - Advanced Streaming and Prediction. ASAP is supposed to learn what TV shows and movies you are most likely to watch, and preload the shows on the device. This eliminates the buffering time from when you select the show to play and the show actually starts playing on your TV.

The voice search of Fire TV is pitched as "voice search that actually works" - you can say the title, genre, actor, director, or whatever you want to search for, and Fire TV promptly brings up the results. Fire TV even saves your voice recordings to get a more accurate match between what you say and what it thinks you said.

No real cons - I love my Fire TV and Fire TV Stick!

HOW DO I WATCH SPORTS?

Live sports broadcasts are one of the few remaining ways for broadcasters to make their money in the traditional way. Since sports fans want to watch their event live, so they can be part of the action and not have the results of their game spoiled because of Internet, you know they're watching the TV at a certain time, and you KNOW they're going to actually watch your commercials, not fast forward through them on a DVR. This is great for cable companies - a captive audience! This is not great for people trying to watch TV without cable.

Here are some of the choices you have for watching sports:

MLB.tv
MLB.tv costs $110 for the regular service and $130 for the premium service. Regular is what a normal fan would expect if they were in the local market, turning on the TV, and watching their team - however, regular only works on a computer. Premium lets you watch the home feed or away feed, have multiple windows open at once, see extra statistics, and has plenty of other features for baseball geeks to feast on. The Premium subscription is required to view MLB.tv through a streaming device. There is a radio-only option of MLB.tv for $20.

The biggest problem with MLB.tv is local blackouts. MLB.tv is only really worth it if you don't live near your team. An extreme example of this is Chicago - if you are a baseball fan in Chicago, and you favorite team is either the Cubs or the White sox, you won't be able to watch either one of them. The radio broadcasts of any games are always available if you are a paid subscriber.

Blackouts do not care if your team is playing at home or away. If you are a San Diego transplant living in Milwaukee, and the Padres are playing the Brewers, the game will be blacked out, even if the game is being played in San Diego.

The other problem is national blackouts. All nationally-televised games are blacked out.

- All postseason games are blacked out.
- The All-Star game is blacked out.
- Most Saturday day games and some night games are blacked out. Blame FOX.
- All Sunday night games are blacked out.

Better to know before you buy, right?

NFL Game Rewind

NFL Game Rewind lets you watch American football games, but only after the game has been played already (that's the "Rewind" part). You cannot watch a live NFL game with NFL Game Rewind.

There are four different packages offered with NFL Game Rewind. The cheapest package is a team package for $29.99, which includes both home and away games for a particular team. The next step up is a Season package, which includes all NFL games during the regular season. The most expensive subscription is Season Plus. Season Plus is all the NFL games including the playoffs and Super Bowl for $69.99.

Although you have to wait until after the game to view the game, NFL Game Rewind has seductive advantages for the busy football fan.

Coaches Film: All-22 and EndZone

The angle you watch football on TV (from the 50 yard line) is not the angle the players see, and it's not the angle the players and coaches review when they're looking at game film. The angle the football players see is from behind the quarterback. These different angles give you a better view of all the players - many times the most interesting action on the field is not where the ball is, or where the quarterback is. Football fans can watch nearly 24 different angles of a play that you cannot find anywhere else.

Past Games
You can watch football games going back to the 2009 season.

Condensed Games
This is extremely helpful if you want to watch a lot of football and you don't have a lot of time. This feature cuts out the timeouts, players walking back to the line of scrimmage, and all the other fluff, leaving pure football. An entire football game can be reduced to 30 minutes.

Telestrator
With a tablet and telestrator, you can mark up a football play like an announcer on TV, with lines and arrows. You can save these plays on your tablet or send them out to your friends.

NFL Game Rewind requires a computer running Microsoft Windows or a tablet.

NBA League Pass
NBA League Pass costs $130 for a five team package and $200 for all team packages. You now have the option to view both home and away game feeds, and watch national broadcasts in the archive of NBA games (neither one of these was possible when League Pass first came out). You are subject to local blackouts - you can only see out of market games that are not nationally televised, which includes playoff games.

NBA League Pass works best with WIRED devices. Wireless devices like Apple TV, Amazon Fire TV Stick, Chromecast, and some Roku devices will suffer frozen streams. Additionally, support for older Rokus ceases whenever the NBA feels like it and the owner of an older Roku will be forced to upgrade to use this service. The stream for NBA League Pass often freezes or fails to load at all. During the commercial breaks, the viewer is presented with a black screen playing loud rock music.

NHL GameCenter Live
NHL GameCenter is $159 a season. The two problems with GameCenter are local blackouts and it is often broken.

Similar to MLB.TV, local teams within a certain radius of your computer are not available on NHL GameCenter. These are normally the games you want to see the most unless you are fortunate enough to be a transplant to a new area. Local games are available on GameCenter after a 48 hour blackout period. Games that appear exclusively on NBCSN or the NHL Network are also blacked out.

NHL GameCenter shows live games, and is available on almost all platforms - desktop, tablet, mobile, Playstation, Xbox, Roku, Apple TV. Sometimes the app works, sometimes it does not. There is often stuttering or lagging of the audio. In 2014, NHL GameCenter stopped working on an older version of Roku, forcing users to upgrade to a new Roku box if they wanted to continue with their subscription. There are also problems using NHL GameCenter consistently with Apple TV.

There is a tape delay with the broadcast stream from NHL GameCenter. This means that if you watch the stream, the video you see and audio you hear will be a few seconds behind the television broadcast (which itself is a few seconds behind the game being played in real life). This is a limitation to be aware of if you participate in on-line activities which require you to be up-to-date to the second.

With GameCenter, you have the ability to watch old games and hide the score of the game - if you're not sure who won, you won't be spoiled when you replay the game. You can watch the game from different angles, and combine multiple games simultaneously on the same screen.

NOW WHAT?

We've gone over a lot of options, and let's do a high level overview once more.

For whatever reason, you are thinking about dropping your cable subscription. There are many options we are familiar with, but we want to watch this stuff on a TV like we're accustomed to. Here are the things that you probably want that will, when used in combination, replace just about everything cable TV used to provide you:

1. An antenna, to view live TV channels in high definition for free
2. One or more streaming services, to watch TV and movies that are not live broadcasts
3. A streaming device to display the streaming services on your TV

It's as simple as that! If you're still not convinced, it is easy to get an antenna from the local store, test it out, and return it if you are dissatisfied. The streaming services are generally on a month-to-month payment plan, so you can test them out on your computer. The cheapest streaming device is the Fire TV Stick at $40, which is also returnable. All these components are cheap and easy to test, and you can do the test while keeping your cable subscription as a backup.

If you haven't already, take a minute and do the math. How much do you pay currently for cable TV? How much will it cost to keep an Internet subscription and start up all the streaming services you want? You can be saving a lot of money!

EPILOGUE

If this book was helpful to you, please leave a review of this book on Amazon! Every review helps!

One last time - for the latest news on streaming services or streaming devices please sign up for updates! It's easiest to keep you informed via email!

To sign up for updates please visit
http://www.toppingspublishing.com/tvwithoutcable

OTHER BOOKS BY RONALD PETER

FIRE TV STICK USER GUIDE: SUPPORT MADE EASY
(http://www.amazon.com/gp/product/B00SGHKGSU)

The Amazon Fire TV Stick is designed to be easy to set up, but let's make sure you're getting the most out of your purchase. You'll learn how to watch movies through Amazon Prime, how to watch movies in your own preexisting movie collection, viewing photos, listening to music, installing official apps, and sideloading apps.

CHROMECAST SETUP: SUPPORT AND USER GUIDE
(http://www.amazon.com/dp/B00T224SQO)

Learn about all the different ways of casting and how to connect Chromecast to TVs in difficult situations, from hotel rooms to airports. Buy this book today on Amazon!